Think it Write it Live it

www.thinkitwriteitliveit.com

Chris Messenger

www.thechrismessenger.com

"The quality of a person's life is in direct proportion to their commitment to excellence" -Vince Lombardi

Most people don't set goals. And of the small percentage that do set goals, most don't know how to go about achieving them, or have a strong enough desire in the first place to really commit to the time and effort it can take to see results. This is why most people don't have what they want.

What if I could show you a way to start with the little things and literally by changing one small habit, create the life you truly WANT and deserve?

Well this is it. You have it in your hands. Now it may not look like much at first (sure at the very core it's a journal) but its what you do with it that can create magic. The very act of habitually writing down what you want, what you are grateful for and purposefully implementing daily actions, can change your entire life.

How do I know? It's a long story, one that I have spent years teaching and promoting as the most effective way to generate habits that lead you to success in any area of life. I have finally come to the conclusion that this information needs to be in everyone's hands. It's through an increased awareness starting with how you think so you can have the life the really want.

Many of the world's most successful people have often attributed their success to how they think. Thoughts followed by the act of writing things down to instill purposeful living into their daily routine is what creates the habits that drive success. Many unsuccessful people in fact, do the opposite- by living moment to moment and never really thinking objectively about the habits they are forming on a daily basis. This is true in friendship, health, success and even finance.

Susan Scott states that 'Everything happens gradually then suddenly'.

So let's slow down the gradual and live PURPOSEFULLY every single day, so the suddenly is favorable and what you WANT.

How does this work? Simple. Each day needs a blueprint. A structured layout of your thoughts and intentions before you set out to take on the day. It's so simple and yet so effective.

STEP 1. GRATITUDE.

One of the most powerful intentions we are capable of and yet one so seldom used. Gratitude is the purposeful act of reflecting on what you are currently grateful for in your life. This single intention is the most important, for when you can truly be grateful FIRST, you can open up your heart, love more freely, forgive easily and live without fear of what may come. This one concept can change your life by instilling the mantra of 'FEEL GOOD NOW'. Become aware of, and focus on what you are grateful for instead of what you don't have.

TIP: This must be a positively focused, emotion based statement that provokes a feeling of happiness, inspiration, love and/or excitement.

STEP 2: PLAN

Next is to write down three actions, three intentions or commitments to set an expectation for a productive day, with proactive steps to work towards your goals. This is a simple process of writing down what you intend to do for the day. Refer to your monthly review page, and write down three specific result-oriented actions you will take in order to move one step closer to those goals.

TIP: Make sure at least one of them scares you. Doing one thing each day that scares you can unconsciously increase your capacity for greatness. It can stretch your skills/abilities and confidence in every way.

STEP 3: POSITIVE REFLECTION

Last is your positive reflection for the day. As you wind down and refer to your three completed actions for the day, reflection is what will cement the learning's and develop a sense of accomplishment and pride. This is critical in training the mind to objectively criticize as well as congratulate and strengthen your developing system, skills, habits and belief.

TIP: This last step cannot be missed. This step ensures you engage in some self-talk raising awareness of how you think. Writing this down will also give you a journal-like view on the year's accomplishments to review often and capture progress in a way our minds are incapable of doing otherwise. This must be positive-focused and evoke love and gratitude for yourself.

I have been fortunate enough to surround myself with some of the world's most successful people and its only through committing myself to the above tasks, which developed my sense of awareness of thoughts, ultimately impacting my daily habits that changed my life. This same gift I now give to you.

THE YEAR AHEAD...

What do I want to achieve this year?

How will I feel when I achieve these goals?

What am I going to change in order to achieve these goals?

" We are what we repeatedly do. Excellence, then, is not an act, but a habit." - Aristotle

Date:

I am so happy and grateful for...

Purposeful actions to achieve my goals...

1.

2.

3.

My positive reflection for today...

"The greatest discovery of my generation is that a human being can alter his life by altering the attitudes of his mind."
– William James

Date:

I am so happy and grateful for...

Purposeful actions to achieve my goals...

1.

2.

3.

My positive reflection for today...

"It is not the strongest of the species that survive, nor the most intelligent, but the one most responsive to change."
— Charles Darwin

Date:

I am so happy and grateful for...

Purposeful actions to achieve my goals...

1.

2.

3.

My positive reflection for today...

"There is no passion to be found playing small - in settling for a life that is less than the one you are capable of living."
- Nelson Mandela

Date:

I am so happy and grateful for…

Purposeful actions to achieve my goals…

1.

2.

3.

My positive reflection for today…

"You've got to win in your mind before you win in your life."
— John Addison

Date:

I am so happy and grateful for…

Purposeful actions to achieve my goals…

1.

2.

3.

My positive reflection for today…

"Life shrinks or expands in proportion to one's courage."
— Anaïs Nin

Date:

I am so happy and grateful for...

Purposeful actions to achieve my goals...

1.

2.

3.

My positive reflection for today...

"The pessimist sees difficulty in every opportunity. The optimist sees the opportunity in every difficulty."
— Winston Churchill

Date:

I am so happy and grateful for…

Purposeful actions to achieve my goals…

1.

2.

3.

My positive reflection for today…

"Our ultimate freedom is the right and power to decide how anybody or anything outside ourselves will affect us."
— Stephen Covey

Date:

I am so happy and grateful for...

Purposeful actions to achieve my goals...

1.

2.

3.

My positive reflection for today...

'Destiny is not a matter of chance, it is a matter of choice; it is not a thing to be waited for, it is a thing to be achieved."
— Winston Churchill

Date:

I am so happy and grateful for...

Purposeful actions to achieve my goals...

1.

2.

3.

My positive reflection for today...

"Your life does not get better by chance, it gets better by change."
– Jim Rohn

Date:

I am so happy and grateful for...

Purposeful actions to achieve my goals...

1.

2.

3.

My positive reflection for today...

"Vision without action is just a dream, action without vision just passes the time, vision with action can change the world"
– Nelson Mandela

Date:

I am so happy and grateful for…

Purposeful actions to achieve my goals…

1.

2.

3.

My positive reflection for today…

"Only those who will risk going too far can possibly find out how far one can go." – T.S. Eliot

Date:

I am so happy and grateful for...

Purposeful actions to achieve my goals...

1.

2.

3.

My positive reflection for today...

"Freedom is not the absence of commitments, but the ability to choose yours." - Paulo Coelho

Date:

I am so happy and grateful for...

Purposeful actions to achieve my goals...

1.

2.

3.

My positive reflection for today...

" I have learned that it's not WHAT I have in my life but WHO I have in my life that counts." - Omer B Washington

Date:

I am so happy and grateful for…

Purposeful actions to achieve my goals…

1.

2.

3.

My positive reflection for today…

" Go confidently in the direction of your dreams. Live the life you have imagined." - Henry David Thoreau

Date:

I am so happy and grateful for…

Purposeful actions to achieve my goals…

1.

2.

3.

My positive reflection for today…

"If you don't design your own life plan, chances are you'll fall into someone else's plan. And guess what they have planned for you? Not much." – Jim Rohn

Date:

I am so happy and grateful for...

Purposeful actions to achieve my goals...

1.

2.

3.

My positive reflection for today...

"Things which matter most must never be at the mercy of things which matter least." - Goethe

Date:

I am so happy and grateful for...

Purposeful actions to achieve my goals...

1.

2.

3.

My positive reflection for today...

"And in the end it's not the years in your life that count. It's the life in your years." – Abraham Lincoln

Date:

I am so happy and grateful for...

Purposeful actions to achieve my goals...

1.

2.

3.

My positive reflection for today...

"Try not. Do or do not. There is no Try." - Yoda

Date:

I am so happy and grateful for...

Purposeful actions to achieve my goals...

1.

2.

3.

My positive reflection for today...

"The only limit to our realization of tomorrow will be our doubts of today." - Franklin D. Roosevelt

Date:

I am so happy and grateful for...

Purposeful actions to achieve my goals...

1.

2.

3.

My positive reflection for today...

"There are no limits on what you can achieve with your life, except the limits you accept in your mind" – Brian Tracy

Date:

I am so happy and grateful for…

Purposeful actions to achieve my goals…

1.

2.

3.

My positive reflection for today…

"Don't be pushed by your problems. Be led by your dreams."
— Ralph Waldo Emerson.

Date:

I am so happy and grateful for…

Purposeful actions to achieve my goals…

1.

2.

3.

My positive reflection for today…

"Either you run the day or the day runs you." – Jim Rohn

Date:

I am so happy and grateful for...

Purposeful actions to achieve my goals...

1.

2.

3.

My positive reflection for today...

"When I thought I couldn't go on, I forced myself to keep going. My success is based on persistence, not luck." – Estee Lauder

Date:

I am so happy and grateful for...

Purposeful actions to achieve my goals...

1.

2.

3.

My positive reflection for today...

"The greatest mistake you can make in life is to be continually fearing you will make one." - Elbert Hubbard

Date:

I am so happy and grateful for…

Purposeful actions to achieve my goals…

1.

2.

3.

My positive reflection for today…

"Action is the foundational key to all success."
— Pablo Picasso

Date:

I am so happy and grateful for...

Purposeful actions to achieve my goals...

1.

2.

3.

My positive reflection for today...

"The secret of getting started is breaking your complex, overwhelming tasks into small manageable tasks, and then starting on the first one." - Mark Twain

Date:

I am so happy and grateful for...

Purposeful actions to achieve my goals...

1.

2.

3.

My positive reflection for today...

"There is only one success – to be able to spend your life in your own way." – Christopher Morley

Date:

I am so happy and grateful for...

Purposeful actions to achieve my goals...

1.

2.

3.

My positive reflection for today...

"Though no one can go back and make a brand new start, anyone can start from now and make a brand new ending."
— Carl Bard

Date:

I am so happy and grateful for…

Purposeful actions to achieve my goals…

1.

2.

3.

My positive reflection for today…

MONTHLY REVIEW

What were my BIG WINS?

How do I feel about these WINS?

What are my GOALS for this month?

"Nothing important was ever achieved without someone taking a chance." - H. Jackson Brown Jr

Date:

I am so happy and grateful for...

Purposeful actions to achieve my goals...

1.

2.

3.

My positive reflection for today...

"I will go anywhere as long as it is forward."
— David Livingston

Date:

I am so happy and grateful for...

Purposeful actions to achieve my goals...

1.

2.

3.

My positive reflection for today...

"Take the first step in faith. You don't have to see the whole staircase, just take the first step." - Martin Luther King Jr

Date:

I am so happy and grateful for…

Purposeful actions to achieve my goals…

1.

2.

3.

My positive reflection for today…

'The greater danger for most of us is not that our aim is too high and we miss it, but that it is too low and we reach it."
— Michelangelo

Date:

I am so happy and grateful for…

Purposeful actions to achieve my goals…

1.

2.

3.

My positive reflection for today…

> *" Many of life's failures are people who did not realize how close they were to success when they gave up."*
> *— Thomas A. Edison.*

Date:

I am so happy and grateful for…

Purposeful actions to achieve my goals…

1.

2.

3.

My positive reflection for today…

"Strive for progress, not perfection." - Unknown

Date:

I am so happy and grateful for...

Purposeful actions to achieve my goals...

1.

2.

3.

My positive reflection for today...

"Twenty years from now you will be more disappointed by the things you didn't do than the ones you did. So, throw off the bowlines. Sail away from the safe harbor. Catch the trade winds in your sails. Explore. Dream. Discover."– Mark Twain

Date:

I am so happy and grateful for...

Purposeful actions to achieve my goals...

1.

2.

3.

My positive reflection for today...

"Life has many ways of testing a person's will, either by having nothing happen at all or by having everything happen all at once."
— Paulo Coelho

Date:

I am so happy and grateful for...

Purposeful actions to achieve my goals...

1.

2.

3.

My positive reflection for today...

"There are two ways of spreading light: to be the candle, or the mirror that reflects it." — Edith Wharton

Date:

I am so happy and grateful for...

Purposeful actions to achieve my goals...

1.

2.

3.

My positive reflection for today...

"With everything that has happened to you, you can either feel sorry for yourself or treat what has happened as a gift. Everything is either an opportunity to grow or an obstacle to keep you from growing. You get to choose." – Dr. Wayne W Dyer

Date:

I am so happy and grateful for...

Purposeful actions to achieve my goals...

1.

2.

3.

My positive reflection for today...

"Believe in yourself! Have faith in your abilities! Without a humble but reasonable confidence in your own powers you cannot be successful or happy." – Norman Vincent Peale

Date:

I am so happy and grateful for...

Purposeful actions to achieve my goals...

1.

2.

3.

My positive reflection for today...

"I've learned that people will forget what you said, people will forget what you did, but people will never forget how you made them feel." – Maya Angelou

Date:

I am so happy and grateful for...

Purposeful actions to achieve my goals...

1.

2.

3.

My positive reflection for today...

" If opportunity doesn't knock, build a door."
— Milton Berle

Date:

I am so happy and grateful for…

Purposeful actions to achieve my goals…

1.

2.

3.

My positive reflection for today…

"Success consists of going from failure to failure without loss of enthusiasm." - Winston Churchill

Date:

I am so happy and grateful for…

Purposeful actions to achieve my goals…

1.

2.

3.

My positive reflection for today…

"If you can dream it, then you can achieve it. You will get all you want in life if you help enough other people get what they want."
— Zig Ziglar

Date:

I am so happy and grateful for...

Purposeful actions to achieve my goals...

1.

2.

3.

My positive reflection for today...

"Surround yourself with only people who are going to lift you higher." - Oprah Winfrey

Date:

I am so happy and grateful for...

Purposeful actions to achieve my goals...

1.

2.

3.

My positive reflection for today...

"We don't see things as they are, we see them as we are."
— Anaïs Nin

Date:

I am so happy and grateful for...

Purposeful actions to achieve my goals...

1.

2.

3.

My positive reflection for today...

"Our greatest weakness lies in giving up. The most certain way to succeed is always to try just one more time."
— Thomas Edison

Date:

I am so happy and grateful for...

Purposeful actions to achieve my goals...

1.

2.

3.

My positive reflection for today...

" Learning is a gift. Even when pain is your teacher."
— Maya Watson

Date:

I am so happy and grateful for...

Purposeful actions to achieve my goals...

1.

2.

3.

My positive reflection for today...

"I've had a lot of worries in my life, most of which never happened." - Mark Twain

Date:

I am so happy and grateful for…

Purposeful actions to achieve my goals…

1.

2.

3.

My positive reflection for today…

"You yourself, as much as anybody in the entire universe, deserve your love and affection." - Buddha

Date:

I am so happy and grateful for...

Purposeful actions to achieve my goals...

1.

2.

3.

My positive reflection for today...

"Hope is a waking dream." - Aristotle

Date:

I am so happy and grateful for...

Purposeful actions to achieve my goals...

1.

2.

3.

My positive reflection for today...

"The past has no power over the present moment."
– Eckhart Tolle

Date:

I am so happy and grateful for…

Purposeful actions to achieve my goals…

1.

2.

3.

My positive reflection for today…

"Happiness is an attitude. We either make ourselves miserable, or happy and strong. The amount of work is the same."
— Francesca Reigler

Date:

I am so happy and grateful for...

Purposeful actions to achieve my goals...

1.

2.

3.

My positive reflection for today...

" If you want light to come into your life, you need to stand where it is shining." - Guy Finley

Date:

I am so happy and grateful for…

Purposeful actions to achieve my goals…

1.

2.

3.

My positive reflection for today…

"Today is a new beginning, a chance to turn your failures into achievements & your sorrows into so goods. No room for excuses." - Joel Brown

Date:

I am so happy and grateful for...

Purposeful actions to achieve my goals...

1.

2.

3.

My positive reflection for today...

" Life is a gift, and it offers us the privilege, opportunity, and responsibility to give something back by becoming more."
— Anthony Robbins

Date:

I am so happy and grateful for...

Purposeful actions to achieve my goals...

1.

2.

3.

My positive reflection for today...

MONTHLY REVIEW

What are my BIG WINS?

How do I feel about these WINS?

What are my GOALS for this month?

" We are all here for some special reason. Stop being a prisoner of your past. Become the architect of your future." – Robin Sharma

Date:

I am so happy and grateful for…

Purposeful actions to achieve my goals…

1.

2.

3.

My positive reflection for today…

> *"Set a goal to achieve something that is so big, so exhilarating that it excites you and scares you at the same time."*
> *— Bob Proctor*

Date:

I am so happy and grateful for...

Purposeful actions to achieve my goals...

1.

2.

3.

My positive reflection for today...

" No matter what the situation, remind yourself I have a choice."
— Deepak Chopra

Date:

I am so happy and grateful for…

Purposeful actions to achieve my goals…

1.

2.

3.

My positive reflection for today…

" All you can change is yourself, but sometimes that changes everything!" - Gary W Goldstein

Date:

I am so happy and grateful for...

Purposeful actions to achieve my goals...

1.

2.

3.

My positive reflection for today...

"The will to win, the desire to succeed, the urge to reach your full potential... these are the keys that will unlock the door to personal excellence." - Confucius

Date:

I am so happy and grateful for...

Purposeful actions to achieve my goals...

1.

2.

3.

My positive reflection for today...

"Take chances, make mistakes. That's how you grow. Pain nourishes your courage. You have to fail in order to practice being brave." - Viktor Frankl

Date:

I am so happy and grateful for...

Purposeful actions to achieve my goals...

1.

2.

3.

My positive reflection for today...

" I am the greatest, I said that even before I knew I was."
— Muhammad Ali

Date:

I am so happy and grateful for…

Purposeful actions to achieve my goals…

1.

2.

3.

My positive reflection for today…

"We are responsible for what we are, and whatever we wish ourselves to be, we have the power to make ourselves."
— Swami Vivekananda

Date:

I am so happy and grateful for...

Purposeful actions to achieve my goals...

1.

2.

3.

My positive reflection for today...

"The difference between stumbling blocks and stepping stones is how you use them." - Napolean Hill

Date:

I am so happy and grateful for…

Purposeful actions to achieve my goals…

1.

2.

3.

My positive reflection for today…

"If someone tells you, "You can't, they really mean" I can't."
— Sean Stephenson

Date:

I am so happy and grateful for…

Purposeful actions to achieve my goals…

1.

2.

3.

My positive reflection for today…

"There is little difference in people, but that little difference makes a big difference. The little difference is attitude. The big difference is whether it is positive or negative."
— W. Clement Stone

Date:

I am so happy and grateful for…

Purposeful actions to achieve my goals…

1.

2.

3.

My positive reflection for today…

" Whatever you want to do, do it now. There are only so many tomorrows." – Michael Landon

Date:

I am so happy and grateful for…

Purposeful actions to achieve my goals…

1.

2.

3.

My positive reflection for today…

"When I do good, I feel good. When I do bad, I feel bad. That's my religion." - Abraham Lincoln

Date:

I am so happy and grateful for…

Purposeful actions to achieve my goals…

1.

2.

3.

My positive reflection for today…

"The difference in winning and losing is most often...not quitting."
— Walt Disney

Date:

I am so happy and grateful for...

Purposeful actions to achieve my goals...

1.

2.

3.

My positive reflection for today...

"You are never too old to set another goal or dream a new dream."
— C.S Lewis

Date:

I am so happy and grateful for…

Purposeful actions to achieve my goals…

1.

2.

3.

My positive reflection for today…

"All things are difficult before they are easy."
— Thomas Fuller

Date:

I am so happy and grateful for...

Purposeful actions to achieve my goals...

1.

2.

3.

My positive reflection for today...

" Success is falling nine times and getting up ten."
— Jon Bon Jovi

Date:

I am so happy and grateful for...

Purposeful actions to achieve my goals...

1.

2.

3.

My positive reflection for today...

"Happiness, like unhappiness, is a proactive choice."
— Stephen Covey

Date:

I am so happy and grateful for...

Purposeful actions to achieve my goals...

1.

2.

3.

My positive reflection for today...

"Be soft. Do not let the world make you hard. Do not let pain make you hate. Do not let the bitterness steal your sweetness. Take pride that even though the rest of the world may disagree, you still believe it to be a beautiful place." – Kurt Vonnegut

Date:

I am so happy and grateful for...

Purposeful actions to achieve my goals...

1.

2.

3.

My positive reflection for today...

"The next time you feel slightly uncomfortable with the pressure in your life, remember no pressure, no diamonds. Pressure is a part of success." - Eric Thomas

Date:

I am so happy and grateful for...

Purposeful actions to achieve my goals...

1.

2.

3.

My positive reflection for today...

" If you can change your mind, you can change your life."
— William James

Date:

I am so happy and grateful for…

Purposeful actions to achieve my goals…

1.

2.

3.

My positive reflection for today…

"When we are no longer able to change a situation, we are challenged to change ourselves." - Viktor Frankl

Date:

I am so happy and grateful for...

Purposeful actions to achieve my goals...

1.

2.

3.

My positive reflection for today...

"Happiness often sneaks in through a door you didn't know you left open." - John Barrymore

Date:

I am so happy and grateful for...

Purposeful actions to achieve my goals...

1.

2.

3.

My positive reflection for today...

"You must do the thing you think you cannot do."
— Eleanor Roosevelt

Date:

I am so happy and grateful for...

Purposeful actions to achieve my goals...

1.

2.

3.

My positive reflection for today...

"If you want to achieve greatness stop asking for permission."
— Eddie Colla

Date:

I am so happy and grateful for...

Purposeful actions to achieve my goals...

1.

2.

3.

My positive reflection for today...

"Things work out best for those who make the best of how things work out." – John Wooden

Date:

I am so happy and grateful for...

Purposeful actions to achieve my goals...

1.

2.

3.

My positive reflection for today...

"To live a creative life, we must lose our fear of being wrong."
— Joseph Chilton Pearce

Date:

I am so happy and grateful for…

Purposeful actions to achieve my goals…

1.

2.

3.

My positive reflection for today…

"If you are not willing to risk the usual you will have to settle for the ordinary." – Jim Rohn

Date:

I am so happy and grateful for…

Purposeful actions to achieve my goals…

1.

2.

3.

My positive reflection for today…

"Trust because you are willing to accept the risk, not because it's safe or certain." - Ritu Ghatourey

Date:

I am so happy and grateful for…

Purposeful actions to achieve my goals…

1.

2.

3.

My positive reflection for today…

"All our dreams can come true if we have the courage to pursue them." - Walt Disney

Date:

I am so happy and grateful for...

Purposeful actions to achieve my goals...

1.

2.

3.

My positive reflection for today...

"Good things come to those who wait, but only the things left by those who hustle." - Abraham Lincoln

Date:

I am so happy and grateful for…

Purposeful actions to achieve my goals…

1.

2.

3.

My positive reflection for today…

"If you do what you've always done, you'll get what you've always got." - Anthony Robbins

Date:

I am so happy and grateful for...

Purposeful actions to achieve my goals...

1.

2.

3.

My positive reflection for today...

"Success is walking from failure to failure with no loss of enthusiasm." – Winston Churchill

Date:

I am so happy and grateful for…

Purposeful actions to achieve my goals…

1.

2.

3.

My positive reflection for today…

"Whenever you see a successful person you only see the public glories, never the private sacrifices to reach them."
— Vaibhav Shah

Date:

I am so happy and grateful for...

Purposeful actions to achieve my goals...

1.

2.

3.

My positive reflection for today...

"Opportunities don't happen, you create them."
— Chris Grosser

Date:

I am so happy and grateful for…

Purposeful actions to achieve my goals…

1.

2.

3.

My positive reflection for today…

"Try not to become a person of success, but rather try to become a person of value." - Albert Einstein

Date:

I am so happy and grateful for...

Purposeful actions to achieve my goals...

1.

2.

3.

My positive reflection for today...

" Great minds discuss ideas; average minds discuss events; small minds discuss people." - Eleanor Roosevelt

Date:

I am so happy and grateful for...

Purposeful actions to achieve my goals...

1.

2.

3.

My positive reflection for today...

"I have not failed. I've just found 10,000 ways that won't work."
— Thomas A. Edison

Date:

I am so happy and grateful for...

Purposeful actions to achieve my goals...

1.

2.

3.

My positive reflection for today...

" No one can make you feel inferior without your consent."
– Eleanor Roosevelt

Date:

I am so happy and grateful for…

Purposeful actions to achieve my goals…

1.

2.

3.

My positive reflection for today…

MONTHLY REVIEW

What were my BIG WINS?

How do I feel about these WINS?

What are my GOALS for this month?

"The whole secret of a successful life is to find out what is one's destiny to do, and then do it." - Henry Ford

Date:

I am so happy and grateful for...

Purposeful actions to achieve my goals...

1.

2.

3.

My positive reflection for today...

"If you're going through hell keep going." – Winston Churchill

Date:

I am so happy and grateful for…

Purposeful actions to achieve my goals…

1.

2.

3.

My positive reflection for today…

"The ones who are crazy enough to think they can change the world, are the ones who do." - Steve Jobs

Date:

I am so happy and grateful for...

Purposeful actions to achieve my goals...

1.

2.

3.

My positive reflection for today...

"What seems to us as bitter trials are often blessings in disguise." - Oscar Wilde

Date:

I am so happy and grateful for…

Purposeful actions to achieve my goals…

1.

2.

3.

My positive reflection for today…

"The meaning of life is to find your gift. The purpose of life is to give it away." - Pablo Picasso

Date:

I am so happy and grateful for...

Purposeful actions to achieve my goals...

1.

2.

3.

My positive reflection for today...

"The distance between insanity and genius is measured only by success." - Bruce Feirstein

Date:

I am so happy and grateful for...

Purposeful actions to achieve my goals...

1.

2.

3.

My positive reflection for today...

"When you stop chasing the wrong things you give the right things a chance to catch you." – Lolly Daskal

Date:

I am so happy and grateful for...

Purposeful actions to achieve my goals...

1.

2.

3.

My positive reflection for today...

"Don't be afraid to give up the good to go for the great."
— John D. Rockefeller

Date:

I am so happy and grateful for…

Purposeful actions to achieve my goals…

1.

2.

3.

My positive reflection for today…

"Do one thing every day that scares you." – Eleanor Roosevelt

Date:

I am so happy and grateful for…

Purposeful actions to achieve my goals…

1.

2.

3.

My positive reflection for today…

"What's the point of being alive if you don't at least try to do something remarkable." - John Green

Date:

I am so happy and grateful for...

Purposeful actions to achieve my goals...

1.

2.

3.

My positive reflection for today...

" Life is not about finding yourself. Life is about creating yourself." - Lolly Daskal

Date:

I am so happy and grateful for...

Purposeful actions to achieve my goals...

1.

2.

3.

My positive reflection for today...

"The mind is everything. What you think, you become."
— *Buddha*

Date:

I am so happy and grateful for...

Purposeful actions to achieve my goals...

1.

2.

3.

My positive reflection for today...

" Innovation distinguishes between a leader and a follower."
— Steve Jobs

Date:

I am so happy and grateful for...

Purposeful actions to achieve my goals...

1.

2.

3.

My positive reflection for today...

"There are two types of people who will tell you that you cannot make a difference in this world: those who are afraid to try and those who are afraid you will succeed." – Ray Goforth

Date:

I am so happy and grateful for...

Purposeful actions to achieve my goals...

1.

2.

3.

My positive reflection for today...

"I find that the harder I work, the more luck I seem to have."
— Thomas Jefferson

Date:

I am so happy and grateful for...

Purposeful actions to achieve my goals...

1.

2.

3.

My positive reflection for today...

"The starting point of all achievement is desire."
— Napolean Hill

Date:

I am so happy and grateful for...

Purposeful actions to achieve my goals...

1.

2.

3.

My positive reflection for today...

"Success is the sum of small efforts, repeated day-in and day-out." - Robert Collier

Date:

I am so happy and grateful for...

Purposeful actions to achieve my goals...

1.

2.

3.

My positive reflection for today...

"If you want to achieve excellence, you can get there today. As of this second, quit doing less-than-excellent work."
— Thomas J. Watson

Date:

I am so happy and grateful for...

Purposeful actions to achieve my goals...

1.

2.

3.

My positive reflection for today...

"Courage is resistance to fear, mastery of fear – not absence of fear." ~Mark Twain

Date:

I am so happy and grateful for…

Purposeful actions to achieve my goals…

1.

2.

3.

My positive reflection for today…

"Only put off until tomorrow what you are willing to die having left undone." - Pablo Picasso

Date:

I am so happy and grateful for...

Purposeful actions to achieve my goals...

1.

2.

3.

My positive reflection for today...

"People often say that motivation doesn't last. Well, neither does bathing - that's why we recommend it daily." - Zig Ziglar

Date:

I am so happy and grateful for...

Purposeful actions to achieve my goals...

1.

2.

3.

My positive reflection for today...

"We become what we think about most of the time, and that's the strangest secret." - Earl Nightingale

Date:

I am so happy and grateful for...

Purposeful actions to achieve my goals...

1.

2.

3.

My positive reflection for today...

"The only place where success comes before work is in the dictionary." - Vidal Sassoon

Date:

I am so happy and grateful for...

Purposeful actions to achieve my goals...

1.

2.

3.

My positive reflection for today...

"It's not what you look at that matters, it's what you see."
– Henry David Thoreau

Date:

I am so happy and grateful for...

Purposeful actions to achieve my goals...

1.

2.

3.

My positive reflection for today...

"Success is liking yourself, liking what you do, and liking how you do it." - Maya Angelou

Date:

I am so happy and grateful for...

Purposeful actions to achieve my goals...

1.

2.

3.

My positive reflection for today...

"As we look ahead into the next century, leaders will be those who empower others." – Bill Gates

Date:

I am so happy and grateful for…

Purposeful actions to achieve my goals…

1.

2.

3.

My positive reflection for today…

"When I dare to be powerful – to use my strength in the service of my vision, then it becomes less and less important whether I am afraid." – Audre Lorde

Date:

I am so happy and grateful for...

Purposeful actions to achieve my goals...

1.

2.

3.

My positive reflection for today...

"Develop success from failures. Discouragement and failure are two of the surest stepping stones to success." – Dale Carnegie

Date:

I am so happy and grateful for…

Purposeful actions to achieve my goals…

1.

2.

3.

My positive reflection for today…

"Don't let the fear of losing be greater than the excitement of winning." - Robert Kiyosaki

Date:

I am so happy and grateful for...

Purposeful actions to achieve my goals...

1.

2.

3.

My positive reflection for today...

MONTHLY REVIEW

What were my BIG WINS?

How do I feel about these WINS?

What are my GOALS for this month?

"You can't connect the dots looking forward; you can only connect them looking backwards. So you have to trust that the dots will somehow connect in your future. You have to trust in something – your gut, destiny, life, karma, whatever. This approach has never let me down, and it has made all the difference in my life." – Steve Jobs

Date:

I am so happy and grateful for…

Purposeful actions to achieve my goals…

1.

2.

3.

My positive reflection for today…

"Successful people do what unsuccessful people are not willing to do. Don't wish it were easier, wish you were better."
— Jim Rohn

Date:

I am so happy and grateful for...

Purposeful actions to achieve my goals...

1.

2.

3.

My positive reflection for today...

"The reason most people never reach their goals is that they don't define them, or ever seriously consider them as believable or achievable. Winners can tell you where they are going, what they plan to do along the way, and who will be sharing the adventure with them." – Denis Watiley

Date:

I am so happy and grateful for…

Purposeful actions to achieve my goals…

1.

2.

3.

My positive reflection for today…

"Success does not consist in never making mistakes but in never making the same one a second time."
— George Bernard Shaw

Date:

I am so happy and grateful for…

Purposeful actions to achieve my goals…

1.

2.

3.

My positive reflection for today…

"You must expect great things of yourself before you can do them." - Michael Jordan

Date:

I am so happy and grateful for...

Purposeful actions to achieve my goals...

1.

2.

3.

My positive reflection for today...

"Motivation is what gets you started. Habit is what keeps you going." – Jim Ryun

Date:

I am so happy and grateful for...

Purposeful actions to achieve my goals...

1.

2.

3.

My positive reflection for today...

"People rarely succeed unless they have fun in what they are doing." - Dale Carnegie

Date:

I am so happy and grateful for…

Purposeful actions to achieve my goals…

1.

2.

3.

My positive reflection for today…

> "There is no chance, no destiny, no fate, that can hinder or control the firm resolve of a determined soul."
> – Ella Wheeler Wilcox

Date:

I am so happy and grateful for...

Purposeful actions to achieve my goals...

1.

2.

3.

My positive reflection for today...

"You've got to get up every morning with determination if you're going to go to bed with satisfaction."
— George Lorimer

Date:

I am so happy and grateful for…

Purposeful actions to achieve my goals…

1.

2.

3.

My positive reflection for today…

"To be successful you must accept all challenges that come your way. You can't just accept the ones you like."
— Mike Gafka

Date:

I am so happy and grateful for…

Purposeful actions to achieve my goals…

1.

2.

3.

My positive reflection for today…

"Success is...knowing your purpose in life, growing to reach your maximum potential, and sowing seeds that benefit others."
— John C. Maxwell

Date:

I am so happy and grateful for…

Purposeful actions to achieve my goals…

1.

2.

3.

My positive reflection for today…

"Be miserable. Or motivate yourself. Whatever has to be done, it's always your choice." - Wayne Dyer

Date:

I am so happy and grateful for...

Purposeful actions to achieve my goals...

1.

2.

3.

My positive reflection for today...

"To accomplish great things, we must not only act, but also dream, not only plan, but also believe."
— Anatole France

Date:

I am so happy and grateful for...

Purposeful actions to achieve my goals...

1.

2.

3.

My positive reflection for today...

"Most of the important things in the world have been accomplished by people who have kept on trying when there seemed to be no help at all." – Dale Carnegie

Date:

I am so happy and grateful for…

Purposeful actions to achieve my goals…

1.

2.

3.

My positive reflection for today…

"You measure the size of the accomplishment by the obstacles you had to overcome to reach your goals."
— Booker T. Washington

Date:

I am so happy and grateful for…

Purposeful actions to achieve my goals…

1.

2.

3.

My positive reflection for today…

> "Little minds are tamed and subdued by misfortune; but great minds rise above it." – Washington Irving

Date:

I am so happy and grateful for…

Purposeful actions to achieve my goals…

1.

2.

3.

My positive reflection for today…

"Don't let what you cannot do interfere with what you can do."
– John R. Wooden

Date:

I am so happy and grateful for…

Purposeful actions to achieve my goals…

1.

2.

3.

My positive reflection for today…

"You may have to fight a battle more than once to win it."
— Margaret Thatcher

Date:

I am so happy and grateful for...

Purposeful actions to achieve my goals...

1.

2.

3.

My positive reflection for today...

"Only he who can see the invisible can do the impossible."
— Frank L. Gaines

Date:

I am so happy and grateful for…

Purposeful actions to achieve my goals…

1.

2.

3.

My positive reflection for today…

"There may be people that have more talent than you, but there's no excuse for anyone to work harder than you do." – Derek Jeter

Date:

I am so happy and grateful for...

Purposeful actions to achieve my goals...

1.

2.

3.

My positive reflection for today...

"Persistence can change failure into extraordinary achievement."
— Marv Levy

Date:

I am so happy and grateful for…

Purposeful actions to achieve my goals…

1.

2.

3.

My positive reflection for today…

"Judge your success by what you had to give up in order to get it." – Dalai Lama

Date:

I am so happy and grateful for...

Purposeful actions to achieve my goals...

1.

2.

3.

My positive reflection for today...

"If at first you don't succeed, you are running about average."
— M.H. Alderson

Date:

I am so happy and grateful for...

Purposeful actions to achieve my goals...

1.

2.

3.

My positive reflection for today...

"Continuous effort — not strength or intelligence — is the key to unlocking our potential." — Liane Cardes

Date:

I am so happy and grateful for…

Purposeful actions to achieve my goals…

1.

2.

3.

My positive reflection for today…

"The difference between the impossible and the possible lies in a person's determination." - Tommy Lasorda

Date:

I am so happy and grateful for…

Purposeful actions to achieve my goals…

1.

2.

3.

My positive reflection for today…

> *"The principle is competing against yourself. It's about self-improvement, about being better than you were the day before."*
> *— Steve Young*

Date:

I am so happy and grateful for...

Purposeful actions to achieve my goals...

1.

2.

3.

My positive reflection for today...

"The mind is the limit. As long as the mind can envision the fact that you can do something, you can do it, as long as you really believe 100 percent." – Arnold Schwarzenegger

Date:

I am so happy and grateful for…

Purposeful actions to achieve my goals…

1.

2.

3.

My positive reflection for today…

"To uncover your true potential you must first find your own limits and then you have to have the courage to blow past them."
— *Picabo Street*

Date:

I am so happy and grateful for…

Purposeful actions to achieve my goals…

1.

2.

3.

My positive reflection for today…

" Without self-discipline, success is impossible, period."
— Lou Holtz

Date:

I am so happy and grateful for…

Purposeful actions to achieve my goals…

1.

2.

3.

My positive reflection for today…

MONTHLY REVIEW

What were my BIG WINS?

How do I feel about these WINS?

What are my GOALS for this month?

If you don't have confidence, you'll always find a way not to win."
— Carl Lewis

Date:

I am so happy and grateful for...

Purposeful actions to achieve my goals...

1.

2.

3.

My positive reflection for today...

> "Obstacles don't have to stop you. If you run into a wall, don't turn around and give up. Figure out how to climb it, go through it or work around it." – Michael Jordan

Date:

I am so happy and grateful for...

Purposeful actions to achieve my goals...

1.

2.

3.

My positive reflection for today...

"Make each day your masterpiece." – John Wooden

Date:

I am so happy and grateful for...

Purposeful actions to achieve my goals...

1.

2.

3.

My positive reflection for today...

"Excellence is the gradual result of always striving to do better."
— Pat Riley

Date:

I am so happy and grateful for...

Purposeful actions to achieve my goals...

1.

2.

3.

My positive reflection for today...

" Win If You Can, Lose If You Must, But NEVER QUIT!"
— Cameron Trammell

Date:

I am so happy and grateful for...

Purposeful actions to achieve my goals...

1.

2.

3.

My positive reflection for today...

"Just keep going. Everybody gets better if they keep at it."
— Ted Williams

Date:

I am so happy and grateful for...

Purposeful actions to achieve my goals...

1.

2.

3.

My positive reflection for today...

" Push yourself again and again. Don't give an inch until the final buzzer sounds." - Larry Bird

Date:

I am so happy and grateful for...

Purposeful actions to achieve my goals...

1.

2.

3.

My positive reflection for today...

"You can't put a limit on anything. The more you dream, the farther you get." – Michael Phelps

Date:

I am so happy and grateful for…

Purposeful actions to achieve my goals…

1.

2.

3.

My positive reflection for today…

"Do not let what you can not do interfere with what you can do."
— John Wooden

Date:

I am so happy and grateful for...

Purposeful actions to achieve my goals...

1.

2.

3.

My positive reflection for today...

"Pain is temporary. It may last a minute, or an hour, or a day, or a year, but eventually it will subside and something else will take its place. If I quit, however, it lasts forever." - Lance Armstrong

Date:

I am so happy and grateful for...

Purposeful actions to achieve my goals...

1.

2.

3.

My positive reflection for today...

"The will to win is important, but the will to prepare is vital."
— Joe Paterno

Date:

I am so happy and grateful for…

Purposeful actions to achieve my goals…

1.

2.

3.

My positive reflection for today…

"Never let your head hang down. Never give up and sit down and grieve. Find another way." – Satchel Paige

Date:

I am so happy and grateful for...

Purposeful actions to achieve my goals...

1.

2.

3.

My positive reflection for today...

"Some people say I have attitude - maybe I do...but I think you have to. You have to believe in yourself when no one else does - that makes you a winner right there." - Venus Williams

Date:

I am so happy and grateful for…

Purposeful actions to achieve my goals…

1.

2.

3.

My positive reflection for today…

"It is not the size of a man but the size of his heart that matters." – Evander Holyfield

Date:

I am so happy and grateful for…

Purposeful actions to achieve my goals…

1.

2.

3.

My positive reflection for today…

" I hated every minute of training, but I said, don't quit. Suffer now and live the rest of your life as a champion."
— Muhammad Ali

Date:

I am so happy and grateful for…

Purposeful actions to achieve my goals…

1.

2.

3.

My positive reflection for today…

"There are only two options regarding commitment. You're either IN or you're OUT. There is no such thing as life in-between."
— Pat Riley

Date:

I am so happy and grateful for...

Purposeful actions to achieve my goals...

1.

2.

3.

My positive reflection for today...

"Never give up! Failure and rejection are only the first step to succeeding." - Jim Valvano

Date:

I am so happy and grateful for...

Purposeful actions to achieve my goals...

1.

2.

3.

My positive reflection for today...

"You miss 100 percent of the shots you don't take."
— Wayne Gretzky

Date:

I am so happy and grateful for...

Purposeful actions to achieve my goals...

1.

2.

3.

My positive reflection for today...

> "I've missed more than 9,000 shots in my career. I've lost almost 300 games. 26 times, I've been trusted to take the game winning shot and missed. I've failed over and over and over again in my life. And that is why I succeed." – Michael Jordan

Date:

I am so happy and grateful for...

Purposeful actions to achieve my goals...

1.

2.

3.

My positive reflection for today...

"Fear and faith both demand you believe in something you cannot see... You choose." – Bob Proctor

Date:

I am so happy and grateful for...

Purposeful actions to achieve my goals...

1.

2.

3.

My positive reflection for today...

" Whatever the mind of man can conceive and believe, it can achieve." - Napoleon Hill

Date:

I am so happy and grateful for…

Purposeful actions to achieve my goals…

1.

2.

3.

My positive reflection for today…

"Strive not to be a success, but rather to be of value."
– Albert Einstein

Date:

I am so happy and grateful for...

Purposeful actions to achieve my goals...

1.

2.

3.

My positive reflection for today...

"Two roads diverged in a wood, and I took the one less traveled by, and that has made all the difference."
— Robert Frost

Date:

I am so happy and grateful for...

Purposeful actions to achieve my goals...

1.

2.

3.

My positive reflection for today...

"I attribute my success to this: I never gave or took any excuse." - Florence Nightingale

Date:

I am so happy and grateful for...

Purposeful actions to achieve my goals...

1.

2.

3.

My positive reflection for today...

"Definiteness of purpose is the starting point of all achievement."
— *W. Clement Stone*

Date:

I am so happy and grateful for...

Purposeful actions to achieve my goals...

1.

2.

3.

My positive reflection for today...

"The past is a ghost, the future a dream. All we ever have is now." - Bill Cosby

Date:

I am so happy and grateful for...

Purposeful actions to achieve my goals...

1.

2.

3.

My positive reflection for today...

"You learn more in failure than you ever do in success."
— Jay Z

Date:

I am so happy and grateful for...

Purposeful actions to achieve my goals...

1.

2.

3.

My positive reflection for today...

"Life is 10% what happens to me and 90% of how I react to it."
— Charles Swindoll

Date:

I am so happy and grateful for...

Purposeful actions to achieve my goals...

1.

2.

3.

My positive reflection for today...

"The most common way people give up their power is by thinking they don't have any." - Alice Walker

Date:

I am so happy and grateful for...

Purposeful actions to achieve my goals...

1.

2.

3.

My positive reflection for today...

MONTHLY REVIEW

What were my BIG WINS?

How do I feel about these WINS?

What are my GOALS for this month?

"It's the repetition of affirmations that leads to belief. And once that belief becomes a deep conviction, things begin to happen." — Muhammad Ali

Date:

I am so happy and grateful for…

Purposeful actions to achieve my goals…

1.

2.

3.

My positive reflection for today…

"The best time to plant a tree was 20 years ago. The second best time is now." - Chinese Proverb

Date:

I am so happy and grateful for...

Purposeful actions to achieve my goals...

1.

2.

3.

My positive reflection for today...

"Eighty percent of success is showing up."
— Woody Allen

Date:

I am so happy and grateful for…

Purposeful actions to achieve my goals…

1.

2.

3.

My positive reflection for today…

"Your time is limited, so don't waste it living someone else's life."
— Steve Jobs

Date:

I am so happy and grateful for...

Purposeful actions to achieve my goals...

1.

2.

3.

My positive reflection for today...

"Winning isn't everything, but wanting to win is."
— Vince Lombardi

Date:

I am so happy and grateful for...

Purposeful actions to achieve my goals...

1.

2.

3.

My positive reflection for today...

"I am not a product of my circumstances. I am a product of my decisions." - Stephen Covey

Date:

I am so happy and grateful for...

Purposeful actions to achieve my goals...

1.

2.

3.

My positive reflection for today...

"You can never cross the ocean until you have the courage to lose sight of the shore." - Christopher Columbus

Date:

I am so happy and grateful for…

Purposeful actions to achieve my goals…

1.

2.

3.

My positive reflection for today…

"Nothing will work unless you do." –Maya Angelou

Date:

I am so happy and grateful for...

Purposeful actions to achieve my goals...

1.

2.

3.

My positive reflection for today...

"Aim for the highest." – Henry Ford

Date:

I am so happy and grateful for...

Purposeful actions to achieve my goals...

1.

2.

3.

My positive reflection for today...

"The two most important days in your life are the day you are born and the day you find out why." – Mark Twain

Date:

I am so happy and grateful for…

Purposeful actions to achieve my goals…

1.

2.

3.

My positive reflection for today…

" Whatever you can do, or dream you can, begin it. Boldness has genius, power and magic in it."
−Johann Wolfgang von Goethe

Date:

I am so happy and grateful for…

Purposeful actions to achieve my goals…

1.

2.

3.

My positive reflection for today…

"The foundation stones for a balanced success are honesty, character, integrity, faith, love and loyalty."
— Zig Ziglar

Date:

I am so happy and grateful for...

Purposeful actions to achieve my goals...

1.

2.

3.

My positive reflection for today...

"Don't judge each day by the harvest you reap but by the seeds that you plant." – Robert Louis Stevenson

Date:

I am so happy and grateful for…

Purposeful actions to achieve my goals…

1.

2.

3.

My positive reflection for today…

> *"If you hear a voice within you say "you cannot paint," then by all means paint and that voice will be silenced."*
> *—Vincent Van Gogh*

Date:

I am so happy and grateful for…

Purposeful actions to achieve my goals…

1.

2.

3.

My positive reflection for today…

"Ask and it will be given to you; search, and you will find; knock and the door will be opened for you." - Jesus

Date:

I am so happy and grateful for…

Purposeful actions to achieve my goals…

1.

2.

3.

My positive reflection for today…

"The only person you are destined to become is the person you decide to be." – Ralph Waldo Emerson

Date:

I am so happy and grateful for…

Purposeful actions to achieve my goals…

1.

2.

3.

My positive reflection for today…

" Go confidently in the direction of your dreams. Live the life you have imagined." -Henry David Thoreau

Date:

I am so happy and grateful for...

Purposeful actions to achieve my goals...

1.

2.

3.

My positive reflection for today...

"When I stand before God at the end of my life, I would hope that I would not have a single bit of talent left and could say, I used everything you gave me." -Erma Bombeck

Date:

I am so happy and grateful for...

Purposeful actions to achieve my goals...

1.

2.

3.

My positive reflection for today...

"Certain things catch your eye, but pursue only those that capture the heart." - Ancient Indian Proverb

Date:

I am so happy and grateful for...

Purposeful actions to achieve my goals...

1.

2.

3.

My positive reflection for today...

"Believe you can and you're halfway there."
— Theodore Roosevelt

Date:

I am so happy and grateful for…

Purposeful actions to achieve my goals…

1.

2.

3.

My positive reflection for today…

"Everything you've ever wanted is on the other side of fear."
— George Addair

Date:

I am so happy and grateful for…

Purposeful actions to achieve my goals…

1.

2.

3.

My positive reflection for today…

"Start where you are. Use what you have. Do what you can."
— Arthur Ashe

Date:

I am so happy and grateful for...

Purposeful actions to achieve my goals...

1.

2.

3.

My positive reflection for today...

"When I was 5 years old, my mother always told me that happiness was the key to life. When I went to school, they asked me what I wanted to be when I grew up. I wrote down 'happy'. They told me I didn't understand the assignment, and I told them they didn't understand life."
― John Lennon

Date:

I am so happy and grateful for…

Purposeful actions to achieve my goals…

1.

2.

3.

My positive reflection for today…

"When one door of happiness closes, another opens, but often we look so long at the closed door that we do not see the one that has been opened for us." – Helen Keller

Date:

I am so happy and grateful for…

Purposeful actions to achieve my goals…

1.

2.

3.

My positive reflection for today…

"Everything has beauty, but not everyone can see."
— Confucius

Date:

I am so happy and grateful for…

Purposeful actions to achieve my goals…

1.

2.

3.

My positive reflection for today…

"How wonderful it is that nobody need wait a single moment before starting to improve the world."
— Anne Frank

Date:

I am so happy and grateful for...

Purposeful actions to achieve my goals...

1.

2.

3.

My positive reflection for today...

" Life is not measured by the number of breaths we take, but by the moments that take our breath away."
— Maya Angelou

Date:

I am so happy and grateful for…

Purposeful actions to achieve my goals…

1.

2.

3.

My positive reflection for today…

"Happiness is not something readymade. It comes from your own actions." - Dalai Lama

Date:

I am so happy and grateful for...

Purposeful actions to achieve my goals...

1.

2.

3.

My positive reflection for today...

" If the wind will not serve, take to the oars."
— Latin Proverb

Date:

I am so happy and grateful for...

Purposeful actions to achieve my goals...

1.

2.

3.

My positive reflection for today...

MONTHLY REVIEW

What were my BIG WINS?

How do I feel about these WINS?

What are my GOALS for this month?

"You can't fall if you don't climb. But there's no joy in living your whole life on the ground." - Dr Seuss

Date:

I am so happy and grateful for…

Purposeful actions to achieve my goals…

1.

2.

3.

My positive reflection for today…

"We must believe that we are gifted for something, and that this thing, at whatever cost, must be attained."
— Marie Curie

Date:

I am so happy and grateful for...

Purposeful actions to achieve my goals...

1.

2.

3.

My positive reflection for today...

"Too many of us are not living our dreams because we are living our fears." - Les Brown

Date:

I am so happy and grateful for…

Purposeful actions to achieve my goals…

1.

2.

3.

My positive reflection for today…

"Challenges are what make life interesting and overcoming them is what makes life meaningful." – Joshua J. Marine

Date:

I am so happy and grateful for…

Purposeful actions to achieve my goals…

1.

2.

3.

My positive reflection for today…

"If you want to lift yourself up, lift up someone else."
— Booker T. Washington

Date:

I am so happy and grateful for...

Purposeful actions to achieve my goals...

1.

2.

3.

My positive reflection for today...

" I have been impressed with the urgency of doing. Knowing is not enough; we must apply. Being willing is not enough; we must do."
— Leonardo da Vinci

Date:

I am so happy and grateful for...

Purposeful actions to achieve my goals...

1.

2.

3.

My positive reflection for today...

"Limitations live only in our minds. But if we use our imaginations, our possibilities become limitless."
— Jamie Paolinetti

Date:

I am so happy and grateful for...

Purposeful actions to achieve my goals...

1.

2.

3.

My positive reflection for today...

"In order to succeed, your desire for success should be greater than your fear of failure." – Bill Cosby

Date:

I am so happy and grateful for...

Purposeful actions to achieve my goals...

1.

2.

3.

My positive reflection for today...

"A person who never made a mistake never tried anything new."
— Albert Einstein

Date:

I am so happy and grateful for…

Purposeful actions to achieve my goals…

1.

2.

3.

My positive reflection for today…

"The person who says it cannot be done should not interrupt the person who is doing it." – Chinese Proverb

Date:

I am so happy and grateful for…

Purposeful actions to achieve my goals…

1.

2.

3.

My positive reflection for today…

"You become what you believe." - Oprah Winfrey

Date:

I am so happy and grateful for...

Purposeful actions to achieve my goals...

1.

2.

3.

My positive reflection for today...

"Build your own dreams, or someone else will hire you to build theirs." - Farrah Gray

Date:

I am so happy and grateful for...

Purposeful actions to achieve my goals...

1.

2.

3.

My positive reflection for today...

" I have learned over the years that when one's mind is made up, this diminishes fear." - Rosa Parks

Date:

I am so happy and grateful for…

Purposeful actions to achieve my goals…

1.

2.

3.

My positive reflection for today…

"It does not matter how slowly you go as long as you do not stop." – Confucius

Date:

I am so happy and grateful for…

Purposeful actions to achieve my goals…

1.

2.

3.

My positive reflection for today…

" If you look at what you have in life, you'll always have more. If you look at what you don't have in life, you'll never have enough." - Oprah Winfrey

Date:

I am so happy and grateful for…

Purposeful actions to achieve my goals…

1.

2.

3.

My positive reflection for today…

"You can't use up creativity. The more you use, the more you have." - Maya Angelou

Date:

I am so happy and grateful for…

Purposeful actions to achieve my goals…

1.

2.

3.

My positive reflection for today…

"Dream big and dare to fail." - Norman Vaughan

Date:

I am so happy and grateful for...

Purposeful actions to achieve my goals...

1.

2.

3.

My positive reflection for today...

"Do what you can, where you are, with what you have."
—Theodore Roosevelt

Date:

I am so happy and grateful for...

Purposeful actions to achieve my goals...

1.

2.

3.

My positive reflection for today...

"Always do your best. What you plant now, you will harvest later." - Og Mandino

Date:

I am so happy and grateful for...

Purposeful actions to achieve my goals...

1.

2.

3.

My positive reflection for today...

"Dreaming, after all, is a form of planning."
— Gloria Steinem

Date:

I am so happy and grateful for...

Purposeful actions to achieve my goals...

1.

2.

3.

My positive reflection for today...

" It's your place in the world; it's your life. Go on and do all you can with it, and make it the life you want to live." - Mae Jemison

Date:

I am so happy and grateful for…

Purposeful actions to achieve my goals…

1.

2.

3.

My positive reflection for today…

"You may be disappointed if you fail, but you are doomed if you don't try." - Beverly Sills

Date:

I am so happy and grateful for…

Purposeful actions to achieve my goals…

1.

2.

3.

My positive reflection for today…

"Expect problems and eat them for breakfast."
— Alfred A. Motapert

Date:

I am so happy and grateful for...

Purposeful actions to achieve my goals...

1.

2.

3.

My positive reflection for today...

" Life is what we make it, always has been, always will be."
— Grandma Moses

Date:

I am so happy and grateful for...

Purposeful actions to achieve my goals...

1.

2.

3.

My positive reflection for today...

"When everything seems to be going against you, remember that the airplane takes off against the wind, not with it." - Henry Ford

Date:

I am so happy and grateful for...

Purposeful actions to achieve my goals...

1.

2.

3.

My positive reflection for today...

"Don't go through life, grow through life."
— Eric Butterworth

Date:

I am so happy and grateful for...

Purposeful actions to achieve my goals...

1.

2.

3.

My positive reflection for today...

" Change your thoughts and you change your world."
— Norman Vincent Peale

Date:

I am so happy and grateful for...

Purposeful actions to achieve my goals...

1.

2.

3.

My positive reflection for today...

"Either write something worth reading or do something worth writing." - Benjamin Franklin

Date:

I am so happy and grateful for...

Purposeful actions to achieve my goals...

1.

2.

3.

My positive reflection for today...

" Nothing is impossible, the word itself says," I'm possible!"
— Audrey Hepburn

Date:

I am so happy and grateful for...

Purposeful actions to achieve my goals...

1.

2.

3.

My positive reflection for today...

MONTHLY REVIEW

What were my BIG WINS?

How do I feel about these WINS?

What are my GOALS for this month?

"The only way to do great work is to love what you do."
— *Steve Jobs*

Date:

I am so happy and grateful for...

Purposeful actions to achieve my goals...

1.

2.

3.

My positive reflection for today...

"There is more pleasure in loving then being loved."
— Thomas Fuller

Date:

I am so happy and grateful for...

Purposeful actions to achieve my goals...

1.

2.

3.

My positive reflection for today...

"The trouble with not having a goal is that you can spend your life running up and down the field and never score."
— Bill Copeland

Date:

I am so happy and grateful for...

Purposeful actions to achieve my goals...

1.

2.

3.

My positive reflection for today...

"You are never too old to set another goal or dream a new dream."
– C. S. Lewis

Date:

I am so happy and grateful for...

Purposeful actions to achieve my goals...

1.

2.

3.

My positive reflection for today...

After a storm comes a calm." - Matthew Henry

Date:

I am so happy and grateful for...

Purposeful actions to achieve my goals...

1.

2.

3.

My positive reflection for today...

"Logic will get you from A to B. Imagination will take you everywhere." - Albert Einstein

Date:

I am so happy and grateful for...

Purposeful actions to achieve my goals...

1.

2.

3.

My positive reflection for today...

" Never leave that till tomorrow which you can do today."
— Benjamin Franklin

Date:

I am so happy and grateful for…

Purposeful actions to achieve my goals…

1.

2.

3.

My positive reflection for today…

" Be not afraid of greatness. Some are born great, some achieve greatness, and some have greatness thrust upon 'em."
— William Shakespeare

Date:

I am so happy and grateful for...

Purposeful actions to achieve my goals...

1.

2.

3.

My positive reflection for today...

"Even if you're on the right track, you'll get run over if you just sit there." - Will Rogers

Date:

I am so happy and grateful for...

Purposeful actions to achieve my goals...

1.

2.

3.

My positive reflection for today...

> *"What lies behind us and what lies before us are tiny matters compared to what lies within us."*
> *— Ralph Waldo Emerson*

Date:

I am so happy and grateful for...

Purposeful actions to achieve my goals...

1.

2.

3.

My positive reflection for today...

"Few are those who see with their own eyes and feel with their own hearts." - Albert Einstein

Date:

I am so happy and grateful for...

Purposeful actions to achieve my goals...

1.

2.

3.

My positive reflection for today...

"With the new day comes new strength and new thoughts."
— Eleanor Roosevelt

Date:

I am so happy and grateful for...

Purposeful actions to achieve my goals...

1.

2.

3.

My positive reflection for today...

"You must be the change you want to see in the world."
— Gandhi

Date:

I am so happy and grateful for...

Purposeful actions to achieve my goals...

1.

2.

3.

My positive reflection for today...

"Remember that happiness is a way of travel, not a destination."
— Roy Goodman

Date:

I am so happy and grateful for…

Purposeful actions to achieve my goals…

1.

2.

3.

My positive reflection for today…

" In between goals is a thing called life, that has to be lived and enjoyed." - Sid Caesar

Date:

I am so happy and grateful for...

Purposeful actions to achieve my goals...

1.

2.

3.

My positive reflection for today...

We see things not as they are, but as we are."
— H. M. Tomlinson

Date:

I am so happy and grateful for…

Purposeful actions to achieve my goals…

1.

2.

3.

My positive reflection for today…

"Vision without action is daydream. Action without vision is nightmare." – Japanese Proverb

Date:

I am so happy and grateful for…

Purposeful actions to achieve my goals…

1.

2.

3.

My positive reflection for today…

"The best way to predict the future is to create it."
— Abraham Lincoln

Date:

I am so happy and grateful for…

Purposeful actions to achieve my goals…

1.

2.

3.

My positive reflection for today…

"Optimism is the faith that leads to achievement. Nothing can be done without hope and confidence." - Helen Keller

Date:

I am so happy and grateful for...

Purposeful actions to achieve my goals...

1.

2.

3.

My positive reflection for today...

"Positive anything is better than negative thinking."
— Elbert Hubbard

Date:

I am so happy and grateful for…

Purposeful actions to achieve my goals…

1.

2.

3.

My positive reflection for today…

" In any situation, the best thing you can do is the right thing; the next best thing you can do is the wrong thing; the worst thing you can do is nothing." - Theodore Roosevelt

Date:

I am so happy and grateful for…

Purposeful actions to achieve my goals…

1.

2.

3.

My positive reflection for today…

"Keep on going and the chances are you will stumble on something, perhaps when you are least expecting it. I have never heard of anyone stumbling on something sitting down." – Charles F. Kettering

Date:

I am so happy and grateful for…

Purposeful actions to achieve my goals…

1.

2.

3.

My positive reflection for today…

"There are two primary choices in life: to accept conditions as they exist, or accept the responsibility for changing them."
— Dr. Denis Waitley

Date:

I am so happy and grateful for...

Purposeful actions to achieve my goals...

1.

2.

3.

My positive reflection for today...

"Stay in chare of you, don't let the outside world control you"
— Bob Proctor

Date:

I am so happy and grateful for…

Purposeful actions to achieve my goals…

1.

2.

3.

My positive reflection for today…

"Don't let life discourage you; everyone who got where he is had to begin where he was." – Richard L. Evans

Date:

I am so happy and grateful for…

Purposeful actions to achieve my goals…

1.

2.

3.

My positive reflection for today…

"If you want to make your dreams come true, the first thing you have to do is wake up." – J.M. Power

Date:

I am so happy and grateful for…

Purposeful actions to achieve my goals…

1.

2.

3.

My positive reflection for today…

"Learn from the past, set vivid, detailed goals for the future and live in the only moment of time over which you have any control: now." - Denis Waitley

Date:

I am so happy and grateful for...

Purposeful actions to achieve my goals...

1.

2.

3.

My positive reflection for today...

"Winners lose much more often than losers. So if you keep losing but you're still trying, keep it up! You're right on track."
— Matthew Keith Groves

Date:

I am so happy and grateful for...

Purposeful actions to achieve my goals...

1.

2.

3.

My positive reflection for today...

"An obstacle is often a stepping stone." - Prescott

Date:

I am so happy and grateful for...

Purposeful actions to achieve my goals...

1.

2.

3.

My positive reflection for today...

"The only thing worse than being blind is having sight but no vision." — Helen Keller

Date:

I am so happy and grateful for…

Purposeful actions to achieve my goals…

1.

2.

3.

My positive reflection for today…

"The real opportunity for success lies within the person and not in the job." - Zig Ziglar

Date:

I am so happy and grateful for...

Purposeful actions to achieve my goals...

1.

2.

3.

My positive reflection for today...

MONTHLY REVIEW

What were my BIG WINS?

How do I feel about these WINS?

What are my GOALS for this month?

Perfection is not attainable, but if we chase perfection we can catch excellence." - Vince Lombardi

Date:

I am so happy and grateful for…

Purposeful actions to achieve my goals…

1.

2.

3.

My positive reflection for today…

" If not us, who? If not now, when?" - John F. Kennedy

Date:

I am so happy and grateful for...

Purposeful actions to achieve my goals...

1.

2.

3.

My positive reflection for today...

"Be more concerned with your character than with your reputation. Your character is what you really are while your reputation is merely what others think you are."
– Dale Carnegie

Date:

I am so happy and grateful for…

Purposeful actions to achieve my goals…

1.

2.

3.

My positive reflection for today…

"The elevator to success is out of order. You'll have to use the stairs... one step at a time." – Joe Girard

Date:

I am so happy and grateful for…

Purposeful actions to achieve my goals…

1.

2.

3.

My positive reflection for today…

"Some men see things as they are and say why – I dream things that never were and say why not." – George Bernard Shaw

Date:

I am so happy and grateful for...

Purposeful actions to achieve my goals...

1.

2.

3.

My positive reflection for today...

"I don't know the key to success, but the key to failure is trying to please everybody." – Bill Cosby

Date:

I am so happy and grateful for...

Purposeful actions to achieve my goals...

1.

2.

3.

My positive reflection for today...

" Be who you are and say what you feel, because those who mind don't matter and those who matter don't mind."
— Dr. Seuss

Date:

I am so happy and grateful for...

Purposeful actions to achieve my goals...

1.

2.

3.

My positive reflection for today...

"Do not go where the path may lead, go instead where there is no path and leave a trail." - Ralph Waldo Emerson

Date:

I am so happy and grateful for...

Purposeful actions to achieve my goals...

1.

2.

3.

My positive reflection for today...

"Enjoy the little things, for one day you may look back and realize they were the big things." - Robert Brault

Date:

I am so happy and grateful for…

Purposeful actions to achieve my goals…

1.

2.

3.

My positive reflection for today…

" Not everything that can be counted counts, and not everything that counts can be counted." - Albert Einstein

Date:

I am so happy and grateful for...

Purposeful actions to achieve my goals...

1.

2.

3.

My positive reflection for today...

" By failing to prepare, you are preparing to fail."
— Benjamin Franklin

Date:

I am so happy and grateful for…

Purposeful actions to achieve my goals…

1.

2.

3.

My positive reflection for today…

"If you can dream it, you can do it." – Walt Disney

Date:

I am so happy and grateful for…

Purposeful actions to achieve my goals…

1.

2.

3.

My positive reflection for today…

"Choose a job you love, and you will never have to work a day in your life." - Confucius

Date:

I am so happy and grateful for…

Purposeful actions to achieve my goals…

1.

2.

3.

My positive reflection for today…

"The pessimist sees difficulty in every opportunity. The optimist sees the opportunity in every difficulty."
— Winston Churchill

Date:

I am so happy and grateful for...

Purposeful actions to achieve my goals...

1.

2.

3.

My positive reflection for today...

"Great thoughts speak only to the thoughtful mind, but great actions speak to all mankind." - Theodore Roosevelt

Date:

I am so happy and grateful for...

Purposeful actions to achieve my goals...

1.

2.

3.

My positive reflection for today...

"You make a living by what you earn; you make a life by what you give." – Winston Churchill

Date:

I am so happy and grateful for...

Purposeful actions to achieve my goals...

1.

2.

3.

My positive reflection for today...

"The journey of a thousand miles begins with one step."
— Lao Tzu

Date:

I am so happy and grateful for...

Purposeful actions to achieve my goals...

1.

2.

3.

My positive reflection for today...

"What counts is not necessarily the size of the dog in the fight - it's the size of the fight in the dog." - Dwight D. Eisenhower

Date:

I am so happy and grateful for...

Purposeful actions to achieve my goals...

1.

2.

3.

My positive reflection for today...

> "Keep away from people who try to belittle your ambitions. Small people always do that, but the really great makes you feel that you, too, can become great."
> – Mark Twain

Date:

I am so happy and grateful for…

Purposeful actions to achieve my goals…

1.

2.

3.

My positive reflection for today…

"Every truth passes through three stages before it is recognized. In the first, it is ridiculed. In the second, it is opposed. In the third, it is regarded as self evident."
— Arthur Schopenhauer

Date:

I am so happy and grateful for...

Purposeful actions to achieve my goals...

1.

2.

3.

My positive reflection for today...

"The degree of loving is measured by the degree of giving."
— Edwin Louis Cole

Date:

I am so happy and grateful for…

Purposeful actions to achieve my goals…

1.

2.

3.

My positive reflection for today…

" Live as if you were to die tomorrow. Learn as if you were to live forever." – Mahatma Gandhi

Date:

I am so happy and grateful for...

Purposeful actions to achieve my goals...

1.

2.

3.

My positive reflection for today...

"It is our choices, that show what we truly are, far more than our abilities." - J. K Rowling

Date:

I am so happy and grateful for...

Purposeful actions to achieve my goals...

1.

2.

3.

My positive reflection for today...

"You have to learn the rules of the game. And then you have to play better than anyone else." - Albert Einstein

Date:

I am so happy and grateful for...

Purposeful actions to achieve my goals...

1.

2.

3.

My positive reflection for today...

"Every great dream begins with a dreamer. Always remember, you have within you the strength, the patience, and the passion to reach for the stars to change the world." – Harriet Tubman

Date:

I am so happy and grateful for…

Purposeful actions to achieve my goals…

1.

2.

3.

My positive reflection for today…

"Take up one idea. Make that one idea your life – think of it, dream of it, live on that idea. Let the brain, muscles, nerves, every part of your body, be full of that idea, and just leave every other idea alone. This is the way to success." – Swami Vivekananda

Date:

I am so happy and grateful for…

Purposeful actions to achieve my goals…

1.

2.

3.

My positive reflection for today…

"You have to want to succeed as bad as you want to breathe."
— Eric Thomas

Date:

I am so happy and grateful for...

Purposeful actions to achieve my goals...

1.

2.

3.

My positive reflection for today...

MONTHLY REVIEW

What were my BIG WINS?

How do I feel about these WINS?

What are my GOALS for this month?

"Watch your thoughts; they become words. Watch your words; they become actions. Watch your actions; they become habits. Watch your habits; they become character. Watch your character; it becomes your destiny." – Lao-Tze

Date:

I am so happy and grateful for...

Purposeful actions to achieve my goals...

1.

2.

3.

My positive reflection for today...

> "What we think, or what we know, or what we believe is, in the end, of little consequence. The only consequence is what we do."
> – John Ruskin

Date:

I am so happy and grateful for...

Purposeful actions to achieve my goals...

1.

2.

3.

My positive reflection for today...

"Conformity is the jailer of freedom and the enemy of growth."
— John F. Kennedy

Date:

I am so happy and grateful for…

Purposeful actions to achieve my goals…

1.

2.

3.

My positive reflection for today…

"Coming together is a beginning; keeping together is progress; working together is success." – Henry Ford

Date:

I am so happy and grateful for...

Purposeful actions to achieve my goals...

1.

2.

3.

My positive reflection for today...

"The quality of your practice determines the caliber of your performance." - Robin Sharma

Date:

I am so happy and grateful for…

Purposeful actions to achieve my goals…

1.

2.

3.

My positive reflection for today…

"The only people you should try to get even with are those that have helped you." – John E Southard

Date:

I am so happy and grateful for...

Purposeful actions to achieve my goals...

1.

2.

3.

My positive reflection for today...

"Never be bullied into silence. Never allow yourself to be made a victim. Accept no one's definition of your life; define yourself."
— Harvey Fierstein

Date:

I am so happy and grateful for…

Purposeful actions to achieve my goals…

1.

2.

3.

My positive reflection for today…

"Success is something you attract by the person you become."
— Jim Rohn

Date:

I am so happy and grateful for...

Purposeful actions to achieve my goals...

1.

2.

3.

My positive reflection for today...

"Success is not final, failure is not fatal: it is the courage to continue that counts." - Winston Churchill

Date:

I am so happy and grateful for...

Purposeful actions to achieve my goals...

1.

2.

3.

My positive reflection for today...

"The best and most beautiful things in this world cannot be seen or even heard, but must be felt with the heart."
— Helen Keller

Date:

I am so happy and grateful for...

Purposeful actions to achieve my goals...

1.

2.

3.

My positive reflection for today...

" With realization of one's own potential and self-confidence in one's ability, one can build a better world." - Dalai Lama

Date:

I am so happy and grateful for...

Purposeful actions to achieve my goals...

1.

2.

3.

My positive reflection for today...

"Change will not come if we wait for some other person or some other time. We are the ones we've been waiting for. We are the change that we seek." – Barack Obama

Date:

I am so happy and grateful for...

Purposeful actions to achieve my goals...

1.

2.

3.

My positive reflection for today...

"When you find peace within yourself, you become the kind of person who can live at peace with others."
— Peace Pilgrim

Date:

I am so happy and grateful for…

Purposeful actions to achieve my goals…

1.

2.

3.

My positive reflection for today…

"Change is the law of life. And those who look only to the past or present are certain to miss the future."
— *John F. Kennedy*

Date:

I am so happy and grateful for...

Purposeful actions to achieve my goals...

1.

2.

3.

My positive reflection for today...

"Every great dream begins with a dreamer. Always remember, you have within you the strength, the patience, and the passion to reach for the stars to change the world." - Harriet Tubman

Date:

I am so happy and grateful for…

Purposeful actions to achieve my goals…

1.

2.

3.

My positive reflection for today…

"Everyone thinks of changing the world, but no one thinks of changing himself." – Leo Tolstoy

Date:

I am so happy and grateful for...

Purposeful actions to achieve my goals...

1.

2.

3.

My positive reflection for today...

"We are all functioning at a small fraction of our capacity to live fully in its total meaning of loving, caring, creating and adventuring. Consequently, the actualizing of our potential can become the most exciting adventure of our lifetime." – Herbert Ottto

Date:

I am so happy and grateful for…

Purposeful actions to achieve my goals…

1.

2.

3.

My positive reflection for today…

"Whoever is happy will make others happy, too."
— Mark Twain

Date:

I am so happy and grateful for…

Purposeful actions to achieve my goals…

1.

2.

3.

My positive reflection for today…

"Wherever you go, go with all your heart." - Confucius

Date:

I am so happy and grateful for...

Purposeful actions to achieve my goals...

1.

2.

3.

My positive reflection for today...

"Find yourself and express yourself in your own particular way. Express your love openly. Life is nothing but a dream, and if you create your life with love, your dream becomes a masterpiece of art." – Don Miguel Ruiz

Date:

I am so happy and grateful for...

Purposeful actions to achieve my goals...

1.

2.

3.

My positive reflection for today...

"Do you want me to tell you something really subversive? Love is everything it's cracked up to be. That's why people are so cynical about it. It really is worth fighting for, being brave for, risking everything for. And the trouble is, if you don't risk anything, you risk even more." - Erica Jong

Date:

I am so happy and grateful for…

Purposeful actions to achieve my goals…

1.

2.

3.

My positive reflection for today…

"Open your eyes, look within. Are you satisfied with the life you are living?" – Bob Marley

Date:

I am so happy and grateful for...

Purposeful actions to achieve my goals...

1.

2.

3.

My positive reflection for today...

"The biggest mistake people make in life is not trying to make a living at doing what they most enjoy."
— Malcolm Forbes

Date:

I am so happy and grateful for…

Purposeful actions to achieve my goals…

1.

2.

3.

My positive reflection for today…

"Once in awhile it really hits people that they don't have to experience the world in the way that they have been told to."
— Alan Keightley

Date:

I am so happy and grateful for...

Purposeful actions to achieve my goals...

1.

2.

3.

My positive reflection for today...

"Man often becomes what he believes himself to be. If I keep on saying to myself that I cannot do a certain thing, it is possible that I may end by really becoming incapable of doing it. On the contrary, if I have the belief that I can do it, I shall surely acquire the capacity to do it even if I may not have it at the beginning." —Mahatma Gandhi

Date:

I am so happy and grateful for...

Purposeful actions to achieve my goals...

1.

2.

3.

My positive reflection for today...

"What I am actually saying is that we need to be willing to let our intuition guide us, and then be willing to follow that guidance directly and fearlessly." — Shakti Gawain

Date:

I am so happy and grateful for...

Purposeful actions to achieve my goals...

1.

2.

3.

My positive reflection for today...

"You can have everything in life that you want if you will just help enough other people get what they want."
— Zig Ziglar

Date:

I am so happy and grateful for...

Purposeful actions to achieve my goals...

1.

2.

3.

My positive reflection for today...

"Don't ask yourself what the world needs, ask yourself what makes you come alive. And then go and do that. Because what the world needs is people who are alive."
— Howard Thurman

Date:

I am so happy and grateful for...

Purposeful actions to achieve my goals...

1.

2.

3.

My positive reflection for today...

"Thousands of candles can be lighted from a single candle, and the life of the candle will not be shortened. Happiness never decreases by being shared." – Buddha

Date:

I am so happy and grateful for…

Purposeful actions to achieve my goals…

1.

2.

3.

My positive reflection for today…

MONTHLY REVIEW

What were my BIG WINS?

How do I feel about these WINS?

What are my GOALS for this month?

"An individual has not started living until he can rise above the narrow confines of his individualistic concerns to the broader concerns of all humanity." - Martin Luther King Jr.

Date:

I am so happy and grateful for…

Purposeful actions to achieve my goals…

1.

2.

3.

My positive reflection for today…

"Only a life worth lived for others is a life worthwhile."
— Albert Einstein

Date:

I am so happy and grateful for…

Purposeful actions to achieve my goals…

1.

2.

3.

My positive reflection for today…

"Spread love everywhere you go. Let no one ever come to you without leaving happier." - Mother Teresa

Date:

I am so happy and grateful for…

Purposeful actions to achieve my goals…

1.

2.

3.

My positive reflection for today…

" Learn to enjoy every minute of your life. Be happy now. Don't wait for something outside of yourself to make you happy in the future. Think how really precious is the time you have to spend, whether it's at work or with your family. Every minute should be enjoyed and savored." - Earl Nightingale

Date:

I am so happy and grateful for...

Purposeful actions to achieve my goals...

1.

2.

3.

My positive reflection for today...

"The value of life is not in the length of days, but in the use we make of them; a man may live long yet very little."
– Michel de Montaigne

Date:

I am so happy and grateful for…

Purposeful actions to achieve my goals…

1.

2.

3.

My positive reflection for today…

"Enjoy your own life without comparing it with that of another."
— Marquis de Condorcet

Date:

I am so happy and grateful for...

Purposeful actions to achieve my goals...

1.

2.

3.

My positive reflection for today...

"There is no value in life except what you choose to place upon it and no happiness in any place except what you bring to it yourself." – Henry David Thoreau

Date:

I am so happy and grateful for…

Purposeful actions to achieve my goals…

1.

2.

3.

My positive reflection for today…

"What we must decide is perhaps how we are valuable, rather than how valuable we are." – Edgar Z. Friedenberg

Date:

I am so happy and grateful for...

Purposeful actions to achieve my goals...

1.

2.

3.

My positive reflection for today...

"The very best thing you can do for the whole world is to make the most of yourself." - Wallace D Wattles

Date:

I am so happy and grateful for...

Purposeful actions to achieve my goals...

1.

2.

3.

My positive reflection for today...

"Embrace the idea of giving with no thought of getting in return."
— Bob Proctor

Date:

I am so happy and grateful for...

Purposeful actions to achieve my goals...

1.

2.

3.

My positive reflection for today...

" We are all here from some special reason. Stop being a prisoner from your past. Become the architect of your future"
— Robin Sharma

Date:

I am so happy and grateful for…

Purposeful actions to achieve my goals…

1.

2.

3.

My positive reflection for today…

"What you believe has more power then what you dream, wish or hope for. What you believe is what you become."
— Oprah Winfrey

Date:

I am so happy and grateful for...

Purposeful actions to achieve my goals...

1.

2.

3.

My positive reflection for today...

"The more relaxed you become the more creative you become."
— Bob Proctor

Date:

I am so happy and grateful for…

Purposeful actions to achieve my goals…

1.

2.

3.

My positive reflection for today…

"There is no passion to be found playing small in settling for a life that is less tan the one you are capable of living."
— Nelson Mandela

Date:

I am so happy and grateful for...

Purposeful actions to achieve my goals...

1.

2.

3.

My positive reflection for today...

"Do not let what you cannot do interfere with what you can do."
— John Wooden

Date:

I am so happy and grateful for…

Purposeful actions to achieve my goals…

1.

2.

3.

My positive reflection for today…

"Your philosophy of life shapes you more then anything else"
— Anthony Robbins

Date:

I am so happy and grateful for...

Purposeful actions to achieve my goals...

1.

2.

3.

My positive reflection for today...

"It's not whether you get knocked down; it's whether you get up." - Vince Lombardi

Date:

I am so happy and grateful for…

Purposeful actions to achieve my goals…

1.

2.

3.

My positive reflection for today…

" We are all here from some special reason. Stop being a prisoner from your past. Become the architect of your future"
– Robin Sharma

Date:

I am so happy and grateful for…

Purposeful actions to achieve my goals…

1.

2.

3.

My positive reflection for today…

"The way you start your day determines how you live your day"
— Robin Sharma

Date:

I am so happy and grateful for…

Purposeful actions to achieve my goals…

1.

2.

3.

My positive reflection for today…

"You will become as small as your controlling desire: As great as your dominant aspiration." - James Allen

Date:

I am so happy and grateful for...

Purposeful actions to achieve my goals...

1.

2.

3.

My positive reflection for today...

"Be yourself; everyone else is already taken."
— Oscar Wilde

Date:

I am so happy and grateful for…

Purposeful actions to achieve my goals…

1.

2.

3.

My positive reflection for today…

"Whether you think you can or think you can't, you're right."
— Henry Ford

Date:

I am so happy and grateful for...

Purposeful actions to achieve my goals...

1.

2.

3.

My positive reflection for today...

" If you know what you want, if you've made up your mind, if you can see it, feel it, and move toward it in some way every single day... It has to happen" - Mike Dooley

Date:

I am so happy and grateful for...

Purposeful actions to achieve my goals...

1.

2.

3.

My positive reflection for today...

"We are all here from some special reason. Stop being a prisoner from your past. Become the architect of your future"
— Robin Sharma

Date:

I am so happy and grateful for…

Purposeful actions to achieve my goals…

1.

2.

3.

My positive reflection for today…

"Goals are like magnets they'll attract the things that make them come true." - Anthony Robbins

Date:

I am so happy and grateful for…

Purposeful actions to achieve my goals…

1.

2.

3.

My positive reflection for today…

"Don't worry about failures worry about the chances you miss when you don't even try" – Jack Canfield

Date:

I am so happy and grateful for…

Purposeful actions to achieve my goals…

1.

2.

3.

My positive reflection for today…

" Every minute spent worrying about the way things were is a moment stolen from creating the way things can be"
— Robin Sharma

Date:

I am so happy and grateful for…

Purposeful actions to achieve my goals…

1.

2.

3.

My positive reflection for today…

"Dreams aren't what you leave behind when morning comes. They are the stuff that fill your every living moment." – David Cuschieri

Date:

I am so happy and grateful for…

Purposeful actions to achieve my goals…

1.

2.

3.

My positive reflection for today…

" We are all of us stars, and we deserve to twinkle."
— Marilyn Monroe

Date:

I am so happy and grateful for…

Purposeful actions to achieve my goals…

1.

2.

3.

My positive reflection for today…

"Sometimes you will never know the value of a moment until it becomes a memory" – Dr. Seuss

Date:

I am so happy and grateful for...

Purposeful actions to achieve my goals...

1.

2.

3.

My positive reflection for today...

"Happiness can be found, even in the darkest times, if one only remembers to turn on the light." - Albus Dumbledore

Date:

I am so happy and grateful for...

Purposeful actions to achieve my goals...

1.

2.

3.

My positive reflection for today...

"Whatever you do, do it well. Do it so well that when people see you do it they will want to come back and see you do it again and they will want to bring others and show them how well you do what you do." - Walt Disney

Date:

I am so happy and grateful for...

Purposeful actions to achieve my goals...

1.

2.

3.

My positive reflection for today...

" Not all of us can do great things, but we can do small things with great love." - Mother Teresa

Date:

I am so happy and grateful for...

Purposeful actions to achieve my goals...

1.

2.

3.

My positive reflection for today...

"There are only two ways to live your life. One is as though nothing is a miracle. The other is as though everything is a miracle." – Albert Einstein

Date:

I am so happy and grateful for...

Purposeful actions to achieve my goals...

1.

2.

3.

My positive reflection for today...

"Do what you feel in your heart to be right, for you'll be criticized anyway. You'll be damned if you do, and damned if you don't." – Eleanor Roosevelt

Date:

I am so happy and grateful for...

Purposeful actions to achieve my goals...

1.

2.

3.

My positive reflection for today...

"It always seems impossible until it's done."
— Nelson Mandela

Date:

I am so happy and grateful for...

Purposeful actions to achieve my goals...

1.

2.

3.

My positive reflection for today...

> *"What lies behind us and what lies before us are tiny matters compared to what lies within us."*
> *— Ralph Waldo Emerson*

Date:

I am so happy and grateful for…

Purposeful actions to achieve my goals…

1.

2.

3.

My positive reflection for today…

"What you believe has more power then what you dream, wish or hope for. What you believe is what you become."
— Oprah Winfrey

Date:

I am so happy and grateful for…

Purposeful actions to achieve my goals…

1.

2.

3.

My positive reflection for today…

STOP what you are doing, turn around and look at all the incredible progress you have made along the way. Your commitment to yourself and unwavering focus on instilling positive habits into your daily routine is admirable. Now imagine what else you can accomplish just by taking these small steps every single day.

There are no limits… So where do you want to go next?

MY BIG COURAGEOUS GOALS for the year ahead are…

www.ingramcontent.com/pod-product-compliance
Lightning Source LLC
Chambersburg PA
CBHW072322170426
43195CB00048B/2216